THIS PLANET IS DOOMED

by

Sun Ra

KICKS BOOKS
NEW YORK, NEW YORK

Acknowledgement is made to Michael D. Anderson, Executive Director of the Sun Ra Music Archive, for permission to reprint the works herein.

Published in 2011 by Kicks Books
An imprint of Kicks Magazine
PO Box 646 Cooper Station
New York NY 10276

Printed in the United States of America

ISBN: 978-0-9659777-1-5

Editor: Miriam Linna
Design: Patrick Broderick/Rotodesign

www.kicksbooks.com

First Edition

*Thanks to Nick Tosches
and Chris Calhoun*

SUN RA

by

AMIRI BARAKA

I passed through Ra's orbit when they 1st arrived from Chicago into the Loisaida (pre-Latino street signs), early '60s. They swept in, with tales and a frantic grapevine of every which observation.

The Weirdness, Outness, Way Outness, Otherness was immediate. Some space metaphysical philosophical surrealistic bop funk. Some blue pyramid home nigger southern different color meaning hip shit. Ra. Sun Ra.

Then they put on weird clothes, space helmets, robes, flowing capes. They did rituals, played in rituals, evoked lost civilizations, used strangeness to teach us open feeling as intelligence.

In those cellars & lofts, Sun Ra spun a cosmic metaphor. He was a philosopher musician. He used music as language, and image.

His was an historical music. He began himself before he played with Fletcher Henderson, playing alternate piano in the orchestra when Fletcher conducted. In recent years he even brought Fletcher and Duke back with a sweetness and contemporary restatement that was thrilling.

Ra was so far out because he had the true self-consciousness of the Afro American intellectual artist revolutionary. He knew our historic ideology and socio-political consciousness was freedom. It is an aesthetic and social dynamic. We think it is good and beautiful!

Sun Ra's consistent statement, musically and spoken, is that this is a primitive world. Its practices, beliefs, religions are uneducated, unenlightened, savage, destructive, already in the past.

That's why Ra left and returned only to say he left. Into the Future. Into Space. He played Interplanetary Music. He described Angels & Devils At Play. From his Heliocentric vision, Ra's music unfolded; it was always, it seemed always there. What it was. But it let us go into it further, showed us its multiple shapes, its wholeness.

Ra was at the Black Arts in Harlem the 1st program we had. He was always up there with us. Talking. Playing. He was one of the presences preaching expanding black consciousness, as expanding human consciousness.

The Sphinx is half-human, half-animal. It rises in fire as the human soul, BA, the Black Bird.

It was Sun Ra and The Myth Science Arkestra that marched across 125th St. with us the day the Arts opened in Harlem, announcing the '60s cultural revolution and sparking a Black Arts Movement, Poetry, Theater, Music, that complemented the Malcolm X-inspired rise of the new SNCC, Panthers, RNA, CAP, YOBU, and the insurrectionary phase of the Black Liberation Movement.

It was Ra, those weekday evenings at The BARTS, who introduced the so-called "Light Show" the rockers ripped off. With his "Space Organ" with its Pythagorean connection of Sound to Color. A low note, a dark hue. A high note, a bright color. Flashed into the dark theater from Ra's miraculous Space Organ.

Ra was also the pioneer in using various-then weird-electronic instruments. But he used everything. You could characterize one aspect of his music as African, as Indian, Latino, Caribbean, but it was all that as Afro American jazz.

No matter how "far out" the insiders said Ra was in the Harlem streets, he was a rare treat. Likewise on

Stirling Street, Newark, in a vacant lot up the street from our Spirit House, Ra brought a huge crowd one summer. And we bathed and luxuriated in the swelling twilight funk, like we were stretched from here to anythere.

We brought the Arkestra back later for a Mardi Gras Kimako's Blues People put on. "What you gonna do when they push that button?" they chanted, marching up Branford Place up onto a flatbed truck on Broad St.

"Kiss your ass, Kiss your ass, Kiss your ass, Goodbye." The long screaming chord by the whole Arkestra had stopped people in their tracks, like an encounter of the further than 3rd type.

"What you gonna do when they push that button? Kiss your ass, Goodbye!"

At times Ra and his Cosmocentric or Heliocentric or Myth Science or Omniverse Arkestras would raise their music as an expression of strange ritual drama. There were Space Goddesses: June Tyson, Verta Mae Grosvenor, who strode through the music in dances of forgotten language, expressing the ancient continuum of religion and ritual drama.

That was a fundamental expression of Ra's music: a communal consciousness, describing the life before Babel and its mindless tower, as well as prophesying its coming.

The Arkestra was a family whose life was music, a life of philosophy. Many giants moved through it, but there were giants who remained.

Pat Patrick, the great baritonist and multi-reed hipster, was my very good friend. People always told us we looked alike, which was funny to us, even if it was true.

John Gilmore I have always thought is one of the finest and hippest tenor players I know. Plus I have known John since I met Ra. John is always on it, into

Another Kind of signification and expression.

It's true, Trane did cop from John Gilmore. Trane would be the 1st to tell you that, too. He told Gilmore.

Marshall Allen, a giant. There is no alto saxophonist I know today, or generally, hipper than Marshall. That this is not common knowledge is depressing. Sun Ra did the music on a record I produced of my play A Black Mass, a telling of Elijah Muhammad's telling of the myth of Jacoub, the mad black magician who created white people!

After the Newark Mardi Gras, Ra came up to the house. It was a block party, in and out of our basement theater. Ra held court in front of a spectacular spread of classic Afro American cuisine Amina had prepared. A bottle of Courvoisier, diverse friends . . . like the grand salons of advanced civilizations, where philosophers and intellectuals and artists could hold forth in open, pleasurable, serious discussion about the whole world and profound reality.

There was in Ra, and continues to be in his music, the witness of alternatives to all of this and what it's got going on. The evolution of humanity was his theme—from revelation to revelation, immeasurable, revolution to revolution, like heartbeats of truth. The breathing of always.

"We Travel The Space Ways," in that beautiful harmony as song chant, spiritual and scientific. Our bodies, our minds, our worlds, our consciousness, what is, travels the spaceways.

"From planet to planet." Perhaps earth will be evacuated, as Welles and Asimov and Bradbury wrote. The environmentalists could explain.

But also, the tower, the to where? Destiny, but as a constant character of motion and change. When?

We are the creators of Heaven and Hell. Everything you imagine has already been done and can be done.

What you can't even imagine is where Sun Ra begins.

The possible is obvious, what is desired is the impossible. What is not is what drives what is, and transforms it into itself.

What is becomes what is not and what is not becomes what is and what is not.

The future is always here in the past.

"Next stop, Jupiter!"

SUN RA: AFROFUTURISM AND THE SUBOPTIC SHADOW WALTZ

by

BHOB STEWART

"The Bach of lumia—when he arrives—may put us all to shame."

—Thomas Wilfred, 1947

In the mid-1960s, Sun Ra was part of the Umbra group of poets. The group included Lorenzo Thomas, who wrote, "The musicians themselves were as cleverly articulate in words as they were on the bandstand; some, in fact, were poets and writers themselves. Charles Mingus and Sun Ra, both excellent poets and lyricists, spoke in vast but terse metaphors to those who took the time to listen."

Umbra Anthology, 1967-1968 grouped Sun Ra's poems with those of Langston Hughes, Amiri Baraka and Allen Ginsberg. Baraka labeled Sun Ra as "our resident philosopher" of the Black Arts Movement, and the Arkestra provided the music accompaniment to Baraka's 1966 play, *A Black Mass.*

In 1968, Baraka and Larry Neal included Sun Ra poems in their 680-page anthology *Black Fire: An Anthology of Afro-American Writing* (reprinted by Black Classics Press in 2007), compiled to stand as the defining work of the Black Arts Movement.

Beyond the interplanetary theatricality, catch-phrases, *non sequiturs*, science-fictional costumes and kozmic chaos, Sun Ra (1914-1993) was an innovative bandleader, a potent pianist, an electronic keyboard pioneer, a visionary Afrofuturist philosopher, an inventive composer, a prolific recording artist, releasing more than 100 albums totaling over 1000 tunes—*Downbeat* called him "the prophet of modern jazz", and a poet of no small dimension.

When the avant-garde finally arrived, they found that Sun Ra had already been there. "I'm a troubleshooter for the cosmos," said Sun Ra, "sent here by the outer space beings from my home planet, Saturn."

"I am Sun Ra," said he, "Ambassador from the intergalactic regions of the council of outer space... I came from a dream that the black man dreamed long ago. I'm actually a presence sent to you by your ancestors."

Descending to the planet Earth and arriving in Alabama, Herman "Sonny" Blount played piano and wrote ditties as a child, performing in Birmingham while in his teens and touring with his own Sonny Blount Orchestra in the late 1930s. He became known as Sonny Lee and Sonny Ray, which flipped into Le Sonra and finally, Sun Ra.

A WWII conscientious objector, he left the South in 1945, arriving in Chicago where he made his first recordings, as a pianist-arranger with Fletcher Henderson's band at Chicago's Club DeLisa. During the mid-1950s, he launched his own label, Saturn, and brought together a band dressed in purple blazers, white gloves and propeller beanies before making a transition to their signature ancient Egyptian garb. Exiting Chicago in 1961, the Arkestra became regulars at Slug's in New York during the 1960s and a focal point of the Black Arts Movement in 1965.

After Sun Ra's move to Philadelphia in 1968,

he went on to tour Europe, tipping into Africa to perform with the Arkestra at the Eqyptian pyramids, and made an experimental feature film, *Space Is the Place* in 1974.

It was during his *12 Days of Infinity* concerts in Boston in December 1978 that I witnessed Sun Ra's ascent into an unclaimed realm of sight and sound, a new ultra-sensory world driven by a device known as the Outer Space Visual Communicator, a mechanized color organ that took his words and music into a super sensory visceral world that redefined all known concepts of rhythm, imagination, and poetic intent.

My own encounter with the OVC occured in the fall of that year when synchronicity sent me in the direction of the OVC's inventor.

I was walking down Boston's Washington Street when I went past the historic decaying Modern Theatre, built in 1900. Some sort of restoration appeared to be underway, and my curiosity about old theaters prompted me to step into the lobby area. When I introduced myself as a journalist to the two young men standing there, one gave me a tour of the auditorium and told me about the restoration work he was doing in preparation for Sun Ra's upcoming *12 Days of Infinity*.

Just as I was stepping back onto the sidewalk, the other guy walked out with me, speaking softly in a conspiratorial manner so the first fellow would not hear. He explained that I had been talking to the wrong person and said I should instead contact someone named Bill Sebastian. That's how I came to learn about "the planet Earth's first visionary intergalactic instrument," which Sebastian had created to catapult Sun Ra into orbit.

The OVC was a machine of loving grace, but it was

not programmed like a computer, nor was it like the liquid light shows of the 1960s. Instead, it had a human operator, Sebastian himself, who played it like a musical instrument. He had invented the much-vaunted color organ extrapolated by science fiction writers of the 1930s. Music critic Mark Rowland was to write, "Sebastian may be responsible for one of the significant artistic breakthroughs of the 20th century, but so far hardly anyone seems to be noticing." Sun Ra noticed and brought Sebastian aboard his cosmic Arkestra.

Sebastian, it turned out, was a suburban Dallas native who played piano and came north to study politics at MIT during the late 1960s. He became a political activist in the early 1970s, and during that same period, he was a Jonzun Crew keyboardist. But when he heard Sun Ra playing in Boston in 1973, his life changed.

Although he knew nothing about electronics, he spent the next five years and $100,000 constructing the OVC as a way to visualize Sun Ra's sounds. Basically, the OVC was a giant hexagon comprised of many smaller hexagons of translucent white plastic. Behind each of the small white hexagons were colored lights. Cables from that 16-foot high display screen were connected to Sebastian's complex control panel with its keyboard and foot pedals. In 1978, after Sun Ra saw the OVC for the first time in Bill Sebastian's Boston loft, he reflected on the "infinite number of vibratory ratios" and made the inventive light magician a member of the Arkestra's galactic empire.

When I heard Sun Ra sounds saturating the auditorium of the Mass College of Art auditorium, Sebastian was caressing his keyboard at the right side of the stage some distance from the OVC, which was centered directly behind the musicians. I wondered how many people in the audience realized he was using his keyboard to paint with light. How many thought he was another one of the musicians producing sounds?

While I began writing a film column for *Heavy Metal* that same year, Sebastian was struggling to open a midtown Boston arts center, the Space Place, intended as a home base for Sun Ra's interstellar excursions. I went there to interview Sebastian for *Heavy Metal*, and at one point, he allowed me to interact with the OVC. For the September 1980 issue, I researched a history of light shows and color organs, incorporating into it the following account of my oneiric electronic experience, the Space Place face-off with the Tesla-like thaumaturgical wizard of the OVC:

> I stand before Bill Sebastian's towering color organ. It looms over me. Bill and I are alone in the cool daytime darkness of the club interior. He sits at his keyboard. I'm listening to my own reverb as I stand at the microphone on the dance floor, scarred by a million disco hustles of years past.
>
> So I laugh. When Sebastian gives his instantaneous visualization of my laughter, beautiful pop hexagons of color radiating outward, a moving mandala of intense and luminescent blues and reds against a black background, my mind transposes these colored circles into representational imagery of an immense orifice—my own mouth. And when I see this, naturally I laugh into the microphone again, and the laughter booms

into the far corners of the club's upper level. The huge hexagonal screen instantly responds with colors completely different, combinations of colors, greens and blues now, spewing forth like giant geometric guffaws from the throat of God. I'm laughing the Cosmic Giggle at last...

Despite the technology involved (six hundred timing circuits that can sustain an image from one one-hundredth of a second to 20 seconds), the main factor here is personal expression. Sebastian's hands glide over 400 touch-sensitive buttons as he does his "electronic fingerpainting." Sebastian told me, "Out of 30 or 40 groups that I ever played with, there's only a handful, three or four groups, that could really relate to the instrument. Sun Ra and Outer Tube are the most remarkable that way... Sun Ra's music is largely what inspired the way the instrument is designed and constructed." The end result is a synesthesia, high-tech and hard edge, of non-representational graphics unlike anything created by light-show technicians of the past.

Today, the OVC lies rusting amid the pine needles and dampness of a Cape Cod field, a home for squirrel nests. The "cosmic orchestra of the universe" echoes across the galaxy, a shadow waltz in the Suboptic Shadow World. Its bright gamma-ray outbursts have dimmed and winked out but, but not so with the intergalactic word worlds of Sun Ra.

On the following pages, unknown and unheralded Afrofuturist poems emerge from the Shadow World—you, the reader, stand upon the threshold of our endless eternal universe. Join the journey. Space is the place.

Countdown for blast-off! X minus five... four... three... two... X minus one... Fire!

—Bhob Stewart

the player sat in space

as all players do...

this planet is doomed

it just breaks me all up, man
it just breaks me all up—
can't understand a damn bit of it
like man, I gotta get away from it
I gotta get away before they mess up
my mind
before they take my soul, man
I just gotta get away
and blast off in my rocket ship

I come from a better place than this
what in the hell am I here for—
here to keep up with the pricks,
all the narrow-minded hoodlums,
all the big talkers and
big money makers and rackets,
all these prickin' squares around?

hell, no
I gotta blast away
I gotta get away, man
I gotta blast off like a super megatron
rocket on
electro dynamic radiation
I can't stand it, man
I gotta get away!
all these pricks messin' up my mind
all the long cars and all the big green
money
they can take it and shove it

people been givin' me the shaft for ages
people, people ain't nothin'
but a bunch of hoodlums
ain't nothin' but a bunch of prickin'
gangsters,
that's all they are
only thing they understand is a
shotgun shell

well, boy
I got it waitin' for them
I got a super megatron bomb waitin'
for them
if they keep pushing me, they gonna get it
they gonna get it
they gonna get it like
electro dynamic radiation on a
super hydro magnetic strawberry patch
like man, the earth, man
is gonna melt
gonna melt, you hear me?
like man, every time I come down that
road
I always see these earth creatures, man
they seem like
they seem like they just ain't got nothin'
they just ain't got nothin'
they seem like they just crawlin'
they just crawlin'
they just can't get out
they just can't
they just can't get their wings up

and fly, man
they just can't fly

like man, I been flyin' for ages
I been flyin' for ages, man
they tryin' to get like me
they tryin' to get like me, man
but they can't do it
they can't fly
they can't
they can't
they can't ride, man
like man, I can ride
but they can't do nothin' but crawl
they just like a bunch of animals
gossipin' and fightin' wars and
all this super-imposed adulthood
and all this,
all this immaturity, man
it's just,
it's just buggin' the hell outta me
and I just gotta get away from them,
I gotta get away from them
before they mess up my mind
like man, I can't let them do it
I can't let them do it
like all these squares,
all these squares with this
economic system and
sweatin' blood on the job and
runnin' after all this
sex stuff

all these sexual broads that're
commercializin' minds
get 'em right in the bag
that's the earthman's bag
and like, man
I gotta break away from them

sex ain't nothin' but a
it ain't nothin' but a gimmick, man,
that's all it is
just a gimmick
psychiatrists use it to mess peoples'
minds up
broads use it to get money in their
pockets
and guys use to kill people with it
like, man they can have it
they can take it and shove it
every cotton pickin' lousy bit of it
I've had enough of it
they tried to pound that stuff in my head
when I was born
they tried to pound that stuff in the head
when I was comin' up
and like, man I'm understanding
this whole, this whole junk now, man
and it's a square bag
it's a lot of child stuff, man
it's gotta stop
it's gotta stop, man because
it's a threat to the entire universe
and like man, I gotta put a stop to it

I gotta put a stop right to it, man
even if I have to turn this planet
into a cinder sandstorm

this planet is doomed
and if all your wars and revolutions
don't stop
this planet is doomed
doomed forever
into a mass of writhing and sweating
melting and flowing mass of protoplasm
like, man the earthman's gonna know
he's gonna
oh, he's gonna know where he is
like man, I ain't gonna be around to see
him
'cause man, I'm gonna be in my groove
I'm gonna be in my bag
and I'm not gonna be here
I'm gonna be on my own planet
I'm gonna be on my planet
where things are big
powerful
things are more meaningful and
have more significance
the vibratory ratio is like
tenfold compared to this lousy planet
like man, it's now time to blast off
it's now time to set my engines goin' and
push the big button
like man, she's waitin'
waitin' on the platform

five hundred
five hundred feet under the ground
all I have to do is just
press the big button
and like, man
I'm gone
I'm gone, man
earthman can't do a thing to stop me
because the earthman is stupid
the earthman is dumb
he's nowhere
I'm aware of the cosmic vibrations
around him
he can't conceive of it
he can't even get there
he's a square from nowhere
and like, man
he's lost
he's lost, man
I feel sorry for him
because there's no hope for him, man
he keeps fightin' these wars and
fightin' these revolutions and
he ain't gettin' nowhere
he's just square, he's nowhere
don't know what to say for him, man
but like, man
I tried to help him out
I tried to give him some understanding
but like, man, he just wouldn't take it

everybody's just a savage
anything different come along, boy
they just gotta
they just gotta kill it
they just gotta
they gotta show how
big they are
they gotta show how powerful they are
they gotta show how narrow minded and
stupid they are
well that's what they are, man
they just stupid, that's all
they just stupid, man
ain't a damn thing I can do about it
ain't a damn thing they can do about it
but like, man
that's just too bad
too
bad

space age needs

there must be a cosmic
dimension of music
which is attuned
to the space-age needs
of the rulers
as well as the peoples
of the earth

touch the stars

at night I sleep my sleep
and dream my dreams
reach into the darkness
and touch the stars
place them in new places
where I would have them
pattern them into another design
of another tomorrow's destiny

angels & demons

my music sings of the discipline of depths
and darkness of space as matter
and matter of outer space as tone, and it
relates—reaches through the void to stars
beyond the places of thought—worlds
without names

not for earth alone

let me write my music
not for earth alone, but for the worlds
for those in being, those in seeming,
those in creative thoughts where angels
and demons and devils each in each
soul and even the eternal one himself is
beyond me the thoughts I have
what if you are out trooping out of body
even where I am inscrutable is the word
yet underneath it all it's not in conscience
another self hidden not in shame
because sarcastically been on rushing
from its hiding place and taken under its
known this tale this proud, this boastful
braggart of circumstance and dream that
something calls life

the government of death

all in the realm of death is
nothing else but peace
its inhabitants have all received
equal rites
because they received equal rights
that is, the services, personal and
complete,
without prejudice of death

death—
truly a great god of endless victory
after victory
what a kingdom
is the kingdom of death
its inhabitants are
without number
through the ages,
they have entered
with perfect discipline
and unbending loyalty
to the majesty
of the invisible power of
death

all governments
on earth
set up by men
are discriminating
but the government of death is a
pure government
it treats all in an equal manner
it is a startling, revealing picture
of equality for all
and all in the realm of death
is nothing else but
peace

State of the Cosmos

all men are equal on the evil plane
and all men are not equal on the
opposite plane
unless the opposite is considered as
the image of the evil plane
this would be the
live plane
but the same actions would be
committed in reverse
and the end of one would be the end
the other
and the beginning of one would be the
beginning of the other
of course, this applies to the action
there is a different law concerning the
appearance of things
the synchronization of the shadows to
the authorized reality
is a key to the reasonable reality of the
state of the world
disconnection of the shadows from the
so-called authorized reality
and the application of the new
potential through resynchronization of
the shadow
to the unauthorized mind images of the
cosmic idea
is a transformation of the shadow into
the living cosmic multi-self
this is the key to the reasonable reality

of the state of the cosmos
synchronization of the shadows to the
authorized reality is the key to the
reasonable state of the world
the disconnection of the shadows from
the so-called authorized reality and the
application of the new potential through
resynchronization of the shadows to the
unauthorized mind image of the cosmic
ideas of transformation of the shadow
into the living cosmic multi-self
this is they key to the reasonable reality
of the state of the cosmos
the synchronization of the shadows
the synchronization of the shadows
the synchronization of the shadows
the synchronization of the shadows to the
authorized reality is the key to the reason
of the state of the world
the synchronization of the shadows to
the authorized reality is the key to the
reasonable state of the world
the disconnection of the shadows from
the so-called authorized reality and the
application of the new potential through
resynchronization of the shadow to the
unauthorized non-image of the cosmic
idea is a transformation of the shadow
into the living cosmic multi-self
this is the key to the reasonable reality of
the state of the cosmos

stranger from the sky

I am not a fantasy in a real sense
I am a fantasy in a false sense
yet I exist
there are no shadows where I am
because I am the fire of the lightening
and the flame of the sun
my name is the sun
I am the stranger from the sky
far away, farther than the eye can see
is my paradise
a mystical world from outer space

how wide the world

how wide the world,
how vast emotions that wander
with the mind
through all the labyrinth of time
seeking ever for that which is
rightful and true
a staunch pioneer who fights to be free
from the liberty of earth

I am an instrument

I am an instrument
the timbre of my voice flies with the
winds of heaven
I belong to one who is more than a
musician
he is an artist
I live to be his pleasure,
I do not flee from him when he
comes to me
for instruments are not sufficient in
themselves
they are cold and lifeless without the
tortured hands and mind
the artist holds myself tenderly in
his hands
first he touches the strings of my heart
too fine to be in tune with the universe
then suddenly vibrant thoughts
strikes there
and music from the world of time
and space is born

dreams rush to meet me

I pull the veil aside
and scan the depths behind it
peer into truths from untruths,
peer into love from hate,
peer into chasm from abyss
I pull the veil aside
and step through its portals
dreams rush to meet me
and tenderly kiss my brow
they still hit the strings
in a pattern of reason
cut from reason
a wind that blows and sweeps the dust
before it hits the sands of time
that flow first forward then backward
first forward then back
the illusion of it all
this is not life
this is not reality
this is not a word of architectural truth
the missing scandal around which they
seek
to blur my view
my beloved prospective
then the songs begin to put rhythm
with chance
that excites the pulse
that deadens the mind
the unliving dash to their feet
to dance to the ruckus music

until they fall exhausted
still unaware that they are unalive
I lift up the veil and step through its
borders
part of me remains there
when I return to now
and I never think of it
except like today when I see
the sun
the faces of people
or hear the clock strike the hour
life has kissed my brow
and I belong unto life and the living
suddenly I awake from sleep
footsteps pattering upon the rim
of the in between knocking at my window
look down at the streets below
look out into space
look fearful behind me
I see nothing there
nothing meets my eye
no sounds greet my ears
only echoes of that
which awoke me with
footsteps pattering upon the rim
on the edge of the in-between

earth is a hole in space

the scientists have discovered at last that
there are black holes in space
I wrote that some time ago
the earth
is one of those holes
the earth is an inside-out planet
outside-in planet
it's one of the black holes in space
its gravitational pull is all inward
and constructed to the people upon
this planet

the earth is a hole in space
space would be a continuous continuity
if it wasn't for the planets
comets
stars
elementary structure substances
that form a hole of material vacuumatron
to emit the transfers
thus the negative transfers
always reveals
the earth is a hole in space
because if a hole in earth was a non-
existent of the earth principle
because it is surrounded by the walls
of earth

then a hole in space is a non-existent
of the space principle
so that the hole of earth
is the whole
because the earth is surrounded
by the walls of space

planet earth needs a new idea
another way of approach

I guess it would have to be part of history
and history
only repeats itself

death speaks to the Negro

to the Negro
death speaks to the Negro
you are my servants

you are my servants!
in my name

for in the way that Christ is the first
born of the dead,
you, the Negro, are the second born
for you are secondary in all my realm
for I, Death, am the first
and since you are in my name, Negro,
I speak to you

you are my servants!
in my name

for in the same way Christ was the first
born of the dead,
you, the Negro, are the second born
for you are secondary in all my realm
for I, Death, am the first
and since you are in my name, Negro,
I speak to you
and reiterate that only I have the keys
to the gates of death

seek not equality with either white
or any other nation
open your eyes and see
behind their pretended pleasure and
power is only impotence and despair
for every one of their citizens are in
my command
when I call their name, they answer

you are my servants!
in my name

I am strange

I am strange
my mind is tinted with the colors of
madness
they fight in silent furor in the effort to
dissolve each other
I am strange
I have a potent degree of love that is so
unwise
in one world that it is wisdom in another
I am strange
I no longer have respect for hate
for I am stronger than hate
I am contemptuous of both those who
hate and those who destroy
I am not a part of the world which hates
and the world which destroys
I want a better world and not only do I
want a better world
I seek to live a better life
that I might have the right to be a part of
a better world
if I hate and destroy, I have no right to
speak of love
love is greater than hate and I have
chosen love above all else in the world
I am strange
I know a secret
truth

I have a secret rendezvous
the wind touches against my windowpane
"Come with me," it says, "Come with me"
I am a force
you are a force
we are brothers, though I am invisible
I come alive when I am ruffled
no wall can hold me.
nothing can withstand my will.
what is your thought?
what is your desire?
come my brother, you are dear to me
I cannot come to you in full force,
for you are too weak to contain me
I might lift you from around and
frighten you,
at a careless moment, I might drop you
in my jaw that you want me to come to
you,
I cannot approach you in your weakness
I am too strong
come to me
as cautious as you will, I will accept you
for the spirit of man is more like myself
than anything on earth
all the most, I think I am the power for
the spirit of man,
for the spirit of man is strong, no power

on earth is greater
and no world can contain it
it will cover the breadth and the width,
for like I, the wind, an aroused spirit is
greatly to be feared
but weapons that you cast are invisible
only fools seek to harm the wind
and when the fools seek to harm the
brother of the wind
come spirit of man
I will take you to new worlds.
I will take you to inner unseen worlds
created in splendors in anything life
contains
if you are fearful, you will die in your fear
but if you become as I, you will be strong
and do as I
I, the wind, come and go as I choose
and none can stop me

the sound of infinity

co-existence with and not of
co-existence to and not in
co-existence degious like counterpoint
co-existence like the spiral parallel like
tomorrow is from today
as much not of as it is of the idea of
each day stands solidly for itself neither
of between
today is that and the quicks time the
joining point
mediums, soothsayers, the crystal gazers
that speaks of yesterdays eternity,
the lost infinity and gazes into the infinity
of the future
the sound infinity of the universe,
co-existence
the sound infinity of the future,
co-existence
I spoke to someone, some being
a herald of mythical prophecies not yet
told yet to be
spoke of the pioneering power of the
evolution of the multi-mind

the self of me

I've found the meaning
but in my solitary search
I've grown used to solitude
when a person searches
for that which is his own
and that which is an integral part
of him
which you find and claim
indeed I have found the meaning
of being a part of it
and doing so
I became a part
I tried to hide
people should probe
and prod into the complexities
until they find
the self of me
which is theirs to claim

sadly, ruthless space

a gate should be here but there's a wall
try to smash it, shatter it, break it down
on every side enclosed for its an
insurmountable wall
fitfully tall
towering as if to fall
you'll never climb them, it's been tried
but all the many walls disguised as the
sun
instead of your fates so but
sadly ruthless space
escape
watch it
don't touch the walls that will stay in
their linked silence
surely each time more than before
certainty and purpose without purpose
develop wings up there
develop wings or to most
stronger still than anybody's walls
that kind of thought is stronger still
than anybody's walls
that kind of truce and that kind of
wisdom
wings greater than wings
wings greater than walls

in orbit

like to know what it is like on my planet?
well I'll tell you
like man, on my planet it's like
hyper dimension atmospheres
there's nothing like it
it's nothing like the earth at all, man,
it's much bigger than that
you get on my planet, man, you
you just don't know where you're at,
man, you
you just don't know where you're at
you look around you and
you see all these hundred-mile buildings,
man, you just kinda go crazy
you just don't know where you're at, man
just don't know where you're at
you're there, man, but
at the same time, you ain't there
you're somewhere else
just don't know where you're at, man
you just try to figure the whole thing
out, man
you just can't make heads or tails outta
nothing

society?
there's no society there to conform
to, man
it's just a density in the hyperprism of the
universe, man

no one can experience nothing like it
you're just like
in the twilight zone, man
in the twilight zone
like man,
you look around and you try to find
yourself
you can't even find yourself, man
it just seems like
you just can't find nothin'
nothin' to identify with you
you're just out there, man
like man, you're just out there

like the density of the hyperprism, man
deep
big
nothing like the earth
it's unlimited—
unlimited in magnitude and direction
like there's no past, there's no future
there's actually no present
because everything moves in an
infinite number of dimensions
inifinite number of vibratory ratios
like man, you're just trying to find
where the present is
you're just trying to find
where the past is
but man, you just can't find neither one

because everything is
homogenous and isotropic with a
hyperspace mechanism on a concurrent
axis
and nobody can experience nothing
like it
earthman can't experience it
earthman can't even come close to it
like, man
that's where I belong
I belong in a place where
you just ain't got no identity
you just ain't got no identity, man
ain't no society to conform to
you're just exploring and exploring
all the time
there's nobody around that can
get in your way
there's nobody around that can bug you
you're just goin', man
you're just goin' all the time
you ain't walking under no ladders
ain't no black cat crossing your path
you're just goin', man, goin'
you wonder where you're gonna stop
you wonder where you started at
like man, you're just goin' and goin'
all the time
like it's ultra dark and ultra light
at the same time
you just can't make it out
see all these buildings around

wonder where they came from
just wonder where they came from
wonder how they got up there
just lookin' man
just observing
just observing
they just seem to come closer and closer
and yet
they're a hundred miles away
hundreds of miles away
you just can't understand it
can't understand how they got so far away
but yet they're just right up on you

like man
how big are they
you just wonder
how big they are
you just wonder
how can you get there
wonder who else is there with you
but like, man,
there's nobody around
you're just there by yourself
nobody around to bug you
nobody around to give you a hard time
nobody around to brainwash you
you just
you just high, man
you just high
you just
you just right there

you just on the scene, man
you're just on a neutral axis and
concurrent force
nobody can take it away from you
but it just
it's just something that's
it's
it's a
it's a real scene, man, like it's a real
chance
like it's a
like it's a real kick, man
and you're scared at the same time
it frightens you at the same time
at the same time it's a pleasing feeling
and you're scared at the same time
and you wonder what
you don't know what's gonna come
off next
you just don't know what's gonna
come off
you just look around you and
after you get outside the rocket ship
you see all the stars and planets just
shining, man, and you just
you just wonder
you just wonder how
how can a place be like this, man?
so big
powerful
magnitude

you look at the earth and you begin to
visualize
how the earth can be so small and
a place like this could be so big
and the people on the earth fightin'
all these wars
and up here are just altogether different
it's so big it just drowns out a war
war just don't mean nothing
the whole thing is just
big
powerful
nobody can experience nothing like it
earthman can't even get there
earthman don't even know what it is
I know what it is, man
'cause I've seen it all the time
and I just gotta get there, man
I just gotta get there, that's all
I just gotta get there and
and can't let nobody hold me back

I take a few steps forward, man, and
like I see all these vibrations around me,
man
I see all these gamma radiations and all
these
cosmic vibrations
they seem just to bounce everywhere,
man
they just don't go in no particular
direction

they seem to be everywhere
they seem to just fold and
intermix in my
neutral axis
and my vibratory ratio seems to
get the messages from the
onslaughts of the vibratory ratios
around me
man, that's—
that's a real gas, man
that's a real gas
can't experience nothin' like it, man
I just gotta get there, man, that's all
I just gotta get there
I just gotta get away from the earthman
but ain't no earthmen here
matter fact
ain't no man there
ain't no woman there
ain't nobody there
it's just a hyper dimension of a
concurrent coplanar force that
tends to make you
part of the universe
part of the gigantic atmosphere, which
intermixes and becomes
becomes something big and frightening
and
tends to make you
part of it
there ain't nothing like it, man

because nobody can take it away from you
that's the wonderful part about it
nobody can take it away from you
it's just there, man
it's just there
like man, it's just there
like, you look around
and you say
like, man
look what I've been missing
but like, man,
I ain't been missing it
I've been here all the time
I just added one more dimension to it, that's all
I just added one more dimension to it
and like, man
I ain't goin' back to the earth
I'm stayin' right here where I belong
it's where I belong, man
nothing back there on the earth for me
what's on the earth for me?
this is where I belong
and that's where I'm gonna stay
right here
I'm gonna stay here for
I don't know how long
I don't know how long I'll be here
I'll just keep goin', man
I'll just keep goin'
don't know where I'm gonna stop

I’ll just keep going just like the
just like the
just like the universe in orbit
the universe keeps turning
the universe just keeps rotating
there ain’t no stop to it
I’ll do the same thing, man
I’ll just keep turning and rotating
just ain’t no stop to me, man
I’ll just keep going
like, man
I’m in orbit, man
I’m in orbit

casting shadows

I am trying to find myself
find the idea from which I sprang
find the forest where of I know it lives
Find the trees where of I am alike
there are no roots or trees on city
pavements
in blasé minds
let me find trees like myself
the same height as I
the same kind as I
that I might raise my limbs in majesty to
the sky
the same as they
trees of kindred spirit
trees attuned to me
whose leaves rustle with music
soft accompaniment of the winds
trees who do not dwarf me in any way
hiding the sunlight from my face
trees to whom I am not a giant
unalike
alien
strange
casting shadows in their way
trees that are not scrawny
malcontent
inclined to ugliness
trees that are themselves
as I am myself
trees that I can always call
my living friends

the universe sent me

the universe sent me
to converse with you
if there is to hear
listen
but do not listen with your ears alone
you must feel with your intuition sense
it is always the unknowing knowing voice
of the quiet vigilant silence
your intuitional intuition sense
the universe sent me to converse with you
this planet is a perfect place
according to its own decision code
but there still is something missing here
a greater need than all of the rest
a need long-hidden from the earth god's
gaze
a need of giant imperative now
it cannot be
it will not be denied
this need's coordinate would wish desire
I speak to you for nature's sentiment too
another gift to offer you, in music
nature's natural master's creation voice is
one of the bridges to the treasure house
of needs fulfilled
what
and how are you?
I'd send my warmest
greetings from the where of the cosmo
usual

I'm doing what I'm supposed to do
I'm being what I'm supposed to be
it is a strange circumstance
like being upon an alien planet world
all alone
but I'm not alone
there is to hear
even here
there are ears that will listen with minds
so spirit pure, are those
for those who are in tune with nature's
cosmo plan plane design can hear what
untuned ears cannot
and those who hear will know the
meaning
of the natural be-ist
the living
be beast
be-ist
the space, he has many sounds of
be-is-ness
the cache
the unknown acoustics
the outer planes of is-ness and not-ness
are all a part of everything and everything
and the nothingness
see the solemn riddle of the double beast

the lie

gaze in the mirror
to be for that which are near me here,
the lions eye can see
think of this and grasp the helm
of balanced thought and push away the
clutter
and things
the snares
the traps
the gravity of the inner void
someone must show the way
a better way than any other way
that they have known
someone must love them more
than they have ever been loved before
it must be the greatest love
ever sent in the world to be
that is not in the realm of was
they must be taught to learn
that unity of the planet is only now
to die
the common heritage of suffering
and despair
why not let the heritage
of suffering and despair
die instead of them,
separate the unity

from the desire
and make one to be another way of life
yet untried
unsought
yet unknown
a transformation to a greater truth
recognition that all the past
is but the consequence
of the lie

the rockets wind, the blast of space

how beautiful is beauty
how strange can strangeness be
if I am the puny ruler,
I just can not explain this
not a lie of in living
not a lie of in thought,
not a lie of in heart,
not a lie of in love
but desire of splendid dream
if I am not alive enough in thought,
if I am not alive enough to live,
I'm strong enough to push
the past behind me and keep it there
strong enough to hold the prism in
my hand
and shape it to be what I will
I will to live,
I will to see another kind of future
I will to be the future
brutally defeat with my heel and sing
another kind of song
louder than all the distorted noises
up behind the design sweeping up
against
a rub of frustrated mankind
louder than mechanical love songs
louder than hypocritical hosannas to god
louder than the dirges of death

louder than the cries of births and pain
louder than the new joys of man
the ill-timed laughter
louder than the rhythm of skin
in hiding from
the rockets wind, the blast of horns
the wood against mouth
steel against mouth
what say you
will you listen
if they are ugliness
if they are beauty
if they are strange
what say you
will you listen and hear
instead of saying
it's the wind and nothing more

this stagnant place of hate

you have wings—
stretch them
flex them
let them grow
groundage is your fate
unless you free them;
crumble as they are crapped, ill-used,
neglect

fly then—
fly towards wisdoms sun
leave this ordained mausoleum,
this stagnant place of hate and higher
sounding word like freedom and justice
and truth that beat and echo innocently
against the futile walls chained enslaved
hidden from sunlight or green field or
living human face his frustration is here
defeating death
leave this place that's born and trapped
and veiled where roses grow across the
pits of hell
leave this place, none will help you, none
will dare
you have wings; use them

vastless and timeless

a broken bowl
will never know
the perfect self once its shape,
but songs
sung in a moments whim
is never sung the same again
and though the heavens are
as far from man as all that past
there not life
as insensitive as one would think
seeming they are so distant
even if the past
knows all the ways of man
so the vastless and timeless
firmament knows
and being what it is
we should search for truth
that we might know
our true way
or insignificance

casting shadows

I am trying to find myself
find the idea from which I sprang
find the forest where of I know it lives
Find the trees where of I am alike
there are no roots or trees on city
pavements
in blasé minds
let me find trees like myself
the same height as I
the same kind as I
that I might raise my limbs in majesty to
the sky
the same as they
trees of kindred spirit
trees attuned to me
whose leaves rustle with music
soft accompaniment of the winds
trees who do not dwarf me in any way
hiding the sunlight from my face
trees to whom I am not a giant
unalike
alien
strange
casting shadows in their way
trees that are not scrawny
malcontent
inclined to ugliness
trees that are themselves
as I am myself
trees that I can always call
my living friends

we must not say no to ourselves

we must not say no to ourselves
for the greater deed
we must not say *can't*
if it is imperative that we should
we must not synchronize with anything
less than art-wise dignity
it is either that we are cosmic giants of
achievement, or something less than the
greater super self
across the thunder bridge of time
we rush with lightning feet to join
hands with those
the friends of seers who truly say
and truly do

like an artiment

if they saw me
they would not know me
and if the danger
they call themselves my jury
my children
they do not know me
how could they be my children?
I do not know them
I only know what they're supposed
to be
what they're supposed to do
I only know them
as they are to me
in the world they never allow it to be
my children
I wish they were
how different they would be from what
they are today
they use the word and say, "My Father"
like a parrot, they speak
like an artiment
more they seem to be some
hideous idol
some idol that they worship
called Myself
the only god they know is themselves and
the laws they make
the only law they have is the love
for salvation

and death
there is no death
not for my children
they would dare to teach that I let
my children die
that my children die?
I own everything that pertains to life
I can forgive everything that pertains
to life
why should I let my children out to death?
why should I let my children
not be
I love life
I love the children who are alive
they're mine, why shouldn't they live?
I want them to live
if they only knew

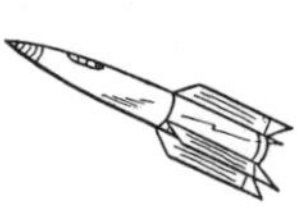

rays strike the earth

this is my day
a sunny day
this is my day
a sunny day
there's so much to give to all bright
beings
striking up the shadows impartially
this is my day
I have so much to say
out of the sun colors come
like spores, the rays strike the earth
and forms of being take shape to be
being raises itself accordingly
to the vibration of the ray to which it
synchronizes itself
invisible light is the ultra light
of darkness
the darkness is the possible light
the all-pervading all
thus the cosmo equation of the light
'cause if the darkness evades the light
so distinguish the meaning of this
an ultra-being
and ultra-being
is all about the music
I always felt
there was something missing
about planet earth
for where are the childhood days

if I search to find out what
then I ran into some things which
couldn't be expressed with words
then I found I needed words again
Then I found I needed
something else
I needed people
not to really listen
but to believe what I'm saying
but as instruments
to be part of the cosmo
cosmic orchestra
of thc universe

so then in my future plans
the people are the instrument

the outer darkness

black is space
the outer darkness
the void direction to the heavens
each spaceport is a heaven
in that, it is a haven
the music of the outer darkness is
the music of the void
the opening is the void
but the opening is synonym to the
beginning
this is an indication interpretation
some music is of specialized
interpretation
some music is of synchronization
precision
every light is a vibrational sight and
sound
it is rhythm and harmony with beams
rays of intensification and projection
visibility
music is light and darkness
precedent of vitality
stimulation extraordinary

black is space
well, sometimes
the outer darkness music
it becomes more than music
the void direction to the heavens
in this thought it reaches an

incredible plane
each spaceport is a heaven
the potential of what can be
in that, it is a haven
done psychically without precedent
the music of the outer darkness is
except in the present designed action
the music of the void
of the eternal endless universe
the opening is the void
every action is rhythm
but the opening is synonym to the
beginning
in all its interrelated being
this is an indication interpretation
I have said before that the music is the
words
some music is of specialized
interpretation
and the words are music
some music is of synchronization
precision
it is all there for you to understand
if you can
every light is a vibrational sight and
sound
and for you to feel, regardless
it is rhythm and harmony with beams
it is a feeling that is a sign of the
being-ness

rays of intensification and projection
visibility
the stimulated movement
music is light and darkness
is the key to on-ness
precedent of vitality
of that which is on
stimulation, extraordinary
still, it is the key

black is space
sometimes music becomes more than music
the outer darkness
and this thought reaches an incredible plane
void direction to the heavens
the potential of what can be
each spaceport is a heaven
done psychically is without precedent
in that, it is a haven
except in the presence-designed action
the music of the outer darkness
of the eternal endless universe
is the music of the void
every action is rhythm
the opening is the void
but the opening is synonym to the beginning
in all its interrelated being
this is an indication interpretation
I have said before that the music is the words and the words are music

some music is of specialized
interpretation
it is all there for you to understand
if you can
some music is of synchronization
precision
and for you to feel, regardless
every light is a vibrational sight and
sound
it is a feeling that is a sign of the
being-ness
it is rhythm and harmony with beams
the stimulated movement
rays of intensification and projection
visibility
is the key to one-ness
music is light and darkness
of that which is on
precedent of vitality
till, it is the key that does not lock
any door
stimulation extraordinary

there is no entrance
there is only the presence of being
where the where-ness dwells
with a coordinating action axis
the knowledge music is different from
the wisdom music
in the finer distinction of presence
wisdom includes intuition
as an ever-present companion

prescience
in a sort of diagonal
symmetrical way
in a way
creation is a transitional form of intuition

black is space
the outer darkness
the void direction to the heavens
each spaceport is a heaven
in that, it is a haven
the music of the outer darkness
is the music of the void
the opening is the void
but the opening is synonym to the
beginning

this is an indication interpretation
some music is of specialized
interpretation
some music is of synchronization
precision
every light is a vibrational sight and
sound
it is rhythm and harmony with beams,
rays of intensification and projection
visibility
music is light and darkness
precedent of vitality
stimulation extraordinary
it must not be forgotten that music is
a language

a language all its own
a language whose foundation and
projection
is melody, rhythm and harmony
the extensions consideration music
in an advanced form
as in composition, sculptures, shape
and form
arrangement, length, depth and width
message, meaning, impression,
strength, degree
beauty, greediness, badness
all dimensions of being
every place, there is music
chaos is music
harmonious peace is music
silence is music
there are different kinds of silences
in silence, there's a world of its own
in a lesser, but not least important sense
silence is an integral part of all music
in a fractional sense
and judged metrically
we must not forget transposition
transposition always results in a change
of color
behold the vastness of the music

once upon a time

time upon time
upon time
upon time
upon time is time
time once upon
once upon is time once
once once once
once upon a time
a time once
upon time a once
once once
upon a time
once once once time
in time in time in the past once
the past
once the past
once time once
the past past the past past
time in time time in time in it time in it
time in it
the in time out out time out time out
comes beyond time beyond time
before a time
before a time is time out
time out time out
there is no time when
time is out time is out
time is out

my world is a space way

my world is a space way
and that's the way to another dimension
of living
the arial concept of being alive
out on the vibrating planes of outer space

my world is a space way
the broad road that never ends
an endless channel
that connects to the worlds upon worlds
of cosmic space
there is the doorway of my world
pause at the threshold, think awhile
before you enter
but once having entered
there is no turning back

science has changed

there are many people
who have sought to make a better world
and that was all right
but they didn't come up with any
equations
for a better world
they had nothing to substitute for the
systems
and the ideas
men can't live in a vacuum
there has to be a better system
to take the place of the systems of
this planet
there has to be a better system to
substitute
for the systems of earth
before the ones that are here
can go
there must be
different kinds of philosophies
different kind of music
different kind of approach to religion
different kind of approach to politics
different kind of approach to an
education
a different kind of approach in
every way
that is the only way
there can be a better world
and everything is based upon the

equations
whether it is good
or bad
you can't get away from the equations
now man is standing upon the threshold
of the greater universe
and everything is changing
potentials
everything is changing
except man
and woman
and child
electronic equipment
astronauts to the moon
cosmonauts
science has changed
everything has changed but man
and woman
and child
someone must show the way
a better way than any way they have
ever known
someone must teach a transformation
to a greater truth
this truth
that is a summation of this planet
Is a bad truth
remember this:
someone must show the way
this is not to convert to leave to persuade

it is of the spirit of the wind
and what does the wind know
it never tells
where does it go?
it never tells
if everyone
is of this planet
why must they disagree as they do?
where did they all come from?
can they prove this is their home?
if this is their home
why do they treat the planet
the way they do?

cosmic eyes

the worship of a statue
can be the worship of the spirit
that inspired the art of the statue
the statue itself is nothing

but the spirit of the statue
is the abstract reality
of the living being
that inspired the creator
to create the image
of the radiating idea
because the idea
is apparent in the visibility of the statue
and those who have cosmic eyes
can see the cosmic meaning projected
through the statue

the damneded air

around the earth
circles the infinity of the damneded air
the damneded inheritance of the earth
are the same vibrations it ever was
we need new air
we need the air that vibrates with the
sound of another kind of mind
we need the beam of the future to strike
the earth
like the lightning and the power of a
thunderbolt
in order that the dying embers of the past
should suddenly be extinct
there is no place for the past in the realm
of the future
except temporarily as an exhibit of that
which is taboo
because the past is the past
and the future is the future
the eternity of the limited past
was for those who were taught the limited
darkness
the unlimited reach of the future is
another kind of forever
there is an inner darkness and there is an
outer darkness
those who become subjects of the inner
darkness dwell therein
those who become subjects of the outer

darkness shall dwell there out
out is the way of the outer
and in, the way of the inner
the in of the inner in
is different from the end of the outer in
because the outer in is the outer on
yes
out is the outer and in is the inner
the way out is the way to living, breathing
life
let's blast the damneded air and claim the
right to be a part of the outer heavens and
outer space
that we might live and breathe and be
eternally alive
forever
let's blast the damnded air
the imprisoning circle that bans the earth
with the echoes of the dead truth of the
damneded word
lets the light shine upon the darkness
that enchains the meaning of the
knowledge that has been used as the law
to destroy

on the outer reach of the unending

when the word was spoken
it was balanced on the pivoting planes of
sound
when it was rhythm
it reflected one plane of sight
in the triple meaning through multi-
division
it was no longer apparent
because the meaning
of the balanced word on the pivoting
planes
cannot be written as it can be thought of
and felt
because the idea of the pivoting planes
is like a touch of vibrating magic
and the magic is the wisdom of ignorance
of unspeakable understanding
intuition
thus is the idea of the pivoting planes
of the greater impossible
and immeasurable equation of space void
reality
on the outer reach of the unending
unknown-ness
we are of the fault that other worlds
seem not to be and yet are
how impossible is the impossible
yet the impossible

is a thought
and every thought is real
an idea
a flash of intuition's fire
a seed of fire that can bring to be
the reality of itself
beyond other thoughts and other worlds
are the potentials
that hidden circumstance and
pretentious chance
cannot control

the past is a dream

the past is a dream
if it is not a dream
where is it now?

the past is a dream
something that came and seemed
to have been
if it is not a dream
where is it now?

the past is a dream
a fictitious fantasy devised
by some sardonic
kindly mind
in the hope that we might see
the meanings of today
and all its possibilities
and then without gratitude
we should not live in such a way
that we might retrogress
to all the mean and lowness
of our imagined yesterdays

the past is a fictitious thing
a one-dimensional fantasy
made to be
a thing to be

in the hope that we might see
beyond the scene
of shadowed past
yes, to see
we must too see
the living beauty
sympathy
the greater alter-universe
is just a place where we should be
this present dream is not the thing
this dream we will
let it not be
this one dimension
fantasy

we are we

I speak of
but I do not speak of
anything
because I speak of everything
I speak of I, but when I speak of me
it is a we
because we are
and that is why we be and am and is
we walk the earth together
and together
we will
and do sail the skies of other clans and
worlds eternal
as me
I am here
but as I
but as I
I am always there
as me, I am here
but as I
I am always there
the somewhere else of there
because of the needs and yearnings of the
us of we

we are small point cosmo infinity pattern
we are *we*
we are so tiny, you see
we are *we*
we belong to the we people
of us

we belong to the we people of us
we are so tiny, you see
see, it is above the realm of kingdom
kingdoms
it is above the realm of kingdom
the kingdoms of time, behold
see the light of another kind of dawn,
behold
behold
come at evenings cast their shadow
before
young light is the shadow of the sun
softly the shadow
lights
upon the land
remember
did you not read
have you not heard yet
about the still-small voice that spoke
interpret beyond the curse
interpret beyond the blessing
if you interpret
listen to their signed interpreter
you cannot follow the same earthworm
path of humanity
and fly with wings of the spirit through
the eternal spheres of being
it is a being
and none of this life you choose to
call life

For this is life
but this is not the kind of being
ultimate utmost of the outer plane
beyond the gravity of the earthbound
Babylonian night
ships sail upon the waters and they go
wherever the wind permits them to go
for the wind is the king of the sea
and the wind is the king of the arid
kingdom
it holds earth like a ball in his hands
it can stop the ships by the power of his
sniff
it can stop the force and movement of
people
by diminishing itself to a thin, invisible,
undetectable weakness
so if the victory through strength is its
greatness
and victory through its weakness is its
lightness
for it is in this measurement
it is a light thing
for light is like the darkness to God
they say
and what is God?

God is the answer to the equation
of the end of man
a word in spite predestination
we look beyond tomorrow

infinity is the language

all created art is music
art
choreography
sculpture
poetry
artworks
photographs
painting
architectural designs found in nature
trees
flowers
grass
every thing's vibration is a different
degree of music
there is music everywhere
infinite infinity is the language of
enduring impression

the sub-dwellers

down in the subterranean places
of the city
down in the catacombs and caverns
of the mind
down
down in the earth
catastrophe
of knowledge
dwell they,
the sub-dwellers

of altered mind
we synchronize to them,
the sub-dwellers
by quickening to us
their potential need
that great emergency within,
cease
they seem like unseated rocks
and roots
hidden from the sun
down
down must go to them
the dawn
the loving heat of the sun
to touch them with remarkable rays
the one wish demands it be –rays –
to envelope them like a net of kindly
prisons
they will be
they will come forward to witness

with the intuition of their own
it is on
it is the voice of the greater universe
that will draw them
to the kinetic vibration of the isthmus
the voice of the greater universe will
draw them
to kinetic vibrations of the isthmus
they will come forward from hence
wherever they are they shall come
forward
to the sound of sounds
yes the sound of sounds will burst of
earth asunder
a projective aim to blast the secret the
cruel citadel
yes even the coded sea will open and
sprawl
and that unknown secret place
will no more be their home
for out of the earth's darkness they
shall come forward
dancing through sound beams of
dark rays of light
and they will rise to the heavens
of the natural skies
there they will be like the fire
of the rays
and the rays
of the sound
of the sun

opposing forces

there were some things
I never tried to do
and most of them
were things I wanted to do
there were these
opposing forces

why should they oppose me?
why?

now, then I thought
there is no such enemy
as I think there are
but then
it is beyond thought
I feel these opposing forces whose power
is their weakness
the power they grant to their servants and
subjects
they exist
indeed they do
I feel and always have felt
it is
it always was
true
since this plane of existence
I came to be
(to know)
they are
(were)

here
I never resisted them
they think I did
it was only pretense
desires I projected to them
these pretense desires I projected to
them
were my non-resistant weapon shield of
defense
I did not desire what they
thought I desired
neither now
nor ever then
non-resistance became my resistance
ny resistance is my non-resistance
do they challenge?
I have already won the victory

how?
we will never know
I am forgetting
I have forgotten how I did
I only know
I know only
I only know
it was never your game
it is always mine
I resist the challenge
foolish foe
I always win the victory

you did not know the secret code
if I win
I win
If I lose
I win
you did not know

you.
do.
not.
know.
there were some things
I never tried to do
and most of them
were things I wanted to do
there were these
opposing forces

why should they oppose me?
why?

now, then I thought
there is no such enemy
as I think there are
but then
it is beyond thought
I feel these opposing forces whose power
is their weakness
the power they grant to their servants and
subjects
they exist

indeed they do
I feel and always have felt
it is
it always was
true
since this plane of existence
I came to be
(to know)
they are
(were)
here
I never resisted them
they think I did
it was only pretense
desires I projected to them
these pretense desires I projected to
them
were my non-resistant weapon
shield of defense
I did not desire what they
thought I desired
neither now
nor ever then
non-resistance became my resistance
my resistance is my non-resistance
do they challenge?
I have already won the victory

how?
we will never know
I am forgetting

I have forgotten how I did
I only know
I know only
I only know
it was never your game
it is always mine
I resist the challenge
foolish foe
I always win the victory
you did not know the secret code
if I win
I win
If I lose
I win
you did not know

you.
do.
not.
know.

strange worlds in my mind

strange
worlds
whirl
in
my
mind
with a glow like sunset and a
pillow-like dawn
strange worlds whirl in my mind
with the living people of the living
dreams
strange dreams in my dream world
a world
awhirl
strange dreams
strange world
awhirl
awhirl
dreams
whirl
awhirl

this universe is endless

this universe is endless
and everything in it is endless
how can it be an endless universe
if everything is not endless?

this universe is endless
and everything in it is endless
how can it be an endless universe
if everything is not endless?

that is a part of it
every beginning is an end
look back and see
it's in the past
every beginning is the end of some
endlessness
look back and see
it's in the past
every beginning is the end of some
endlessness
but the past is an eternity on its own
it is not a part of the endless universe
because the past
had an end
it is the realm of the ended

look backward at the past and
you will see
all the beginnings are there

look backward at the past and
you will see
all the beginnings are there

if you have an end in view
what's your end desire?
be careful
do not make the end you seek
the end
there are different kinds of ends like
book ends are
and book ends are
but book ends end
what does the law of book ends say?
that is the answer of the way

when they are booked
they're in
thc book

planet of death

I gave up my life and am here on
this planet
of death
in order to teach my enemies that their
life is nothing else
but death
and that their planet was isolated from
the cosmic spheres
whence I gave up my life
I gave up my life
not here
but there
now I dwell on this rash planet of death
called by the kind name of earth
I gave up a greater life than anyone here
has ever known
I gave up my heavenly life
now I dwell here on this planet of death
here on this planet of death
they are enchanted by the words of death
and subject to the oath of death
they worship the life of death
and seek death
in order to gain freedom
their liberty is the proclamation of a
soul in famine
yes, death is the proclamation of liberty
the oath of death promises liberty to all
and they are free among the dead

chained to the word of the law of the
beast
how beautiful my world
the world they do not know
how beautiful my world
the world I left behind
out on the outer realm of cosmic
timelessness
is the life I gave and became not to be
in order if I be not
still I am
even though I dwell upon this
isolated planet
of death

message to earthman

hail!

how how how how
how how how how how
how how how how how how how
how
are you?
I
I
I am fine
and it seems that you are going going
going going my way
one day you're gonna take take take this
trip
in the forever ever ever ever rocket ship
this flight is leaving soon
our destination is going going going
high high up up up up up
up to the planets in spite of them
past past past the sky
brother Mars will let you by
old Jupiter will wink his eye
to greater things we'll fly
in our never ever ever rocket ship

never take this trip trip trip
look out look out look out Jake
don't be outside when they close those
red-brick gates

hey Old Joe
how you doing old man Moe?
don't get caught in the door
you might stop feeling that fight
'cause it
take
take
take
away your might

hail
hail
how
 how
  how
   how high is it?
take a trip to the land
come on
come on come on man
close the door

(scream)

as we all beam back for Mars!

in the world of dreams

if all that were
was like a wish,
would I for all
that were

if all there were
is that which never came to be,
would I for all
that were

all that was now
in the world of dreams
bound in thought,
in fruitful reminisce
would I
for all that were,
all that words cannot express
all that dreams can not remember
the enchantment, the warmth, the
rare content;
would I for these
and these alone
that I might live
as my living decree
I should
Before there were an oath of the kingdom
of death;
as once I did before there was a date or
time the world calls now

As before the realm of once I were
before the beginning of the time
of what the world is now
before there was an idea
of enacted play of words
of which a sleeping world
calls law
the law of now

the endless eternal universe

the greatness of any country of people
is music
it is either:
the soul is the music or
the music is the soul
whether or not
a nation
a people
a government
or an individual
whether real or
artificial
schools cannot develop soul
but it can be arranged that surroundings
can be lenient
and more pleasant in their attitudes
toward sound or the creative artist
what can music achieve towards
making this world
a place more livable
music is the constructive spiritual
landscaper
it is to be hoped that the world will
choose
the constructive masteries
instead of the other kind
this decision depends upon
how sensible a nation or nations can be
something else is needed on this planet—
music

which has not really had a chance to
demonstrate its compatibility
to human
or mankind's continuity
it is said that music soothes the savage
beast
sometimes music becomes more than
music
and this far reach is of incredible pain
the potential of what can be done
psychically
is without deceit except in the present
design
of the eternal, endless universe
each in his rhythm
and all its interrelated being
I have said before
that the music is the words
and the words are the music
It is all there for you to understand if you
can
and for you to feel, regardless
It is the feeling that is the sign of the
beingness
the stimulation
movement is the key to the one-ness
Of that which is one
still, it is a key that does not fit any door
there is no entrance
there is only the presence

be prepared , aware
hear the coordinated action
knowledge music is different from
wisdom music
in the finer distinction
wisdom improves intuition
as an ever-present companion
in a diagonal, circumtropical way
weight creation is a transitional form
of intuition

it must not be forgotten that music
is a language unto its own
a language through sound-based
projection is melody
rhythm, and
harmony
the extension
consideration of music in advanced form
as to compositional sculpture
shape and form
arrangement
depth and width
message meaning impression
strength, degree, duty
badness
all dimensions of being
every place that is music
chaos is music and harmonious peace is
music

silence is music
there are different kinds of silences
each silence is a world of its own
in a lesser
but not least important sense
silence is an integral part of all music
in a fractional sense when judged
metrically
we must not forget transposition
transposition always results
in a change of color
behold the vastness of the music
it is as vast as the greater all-ness and the
greater never-ness
music and its metaphases
must not be ignored
are you thinking of metaphysics alone?
well, don't
in the future
and even as of now
you will have to pretend
and recognize
the retromental and
mental spirit
also, you will see
the blue metathesis

music is a science
too long ignored

light from other worlds

I have forgotten
the old ways
the old paths
I seek
I seek a new way
not like this new place of one dimension
not like this place
this place of shame confused with glory
but a vaster realm
of profitable enlightened vision
a region of chromatic truths
abstracts of living design
full of warmth
and sundry planes of light from other
worlds
and sundry planes of light from other
worlds

man and planet earth

the planet is the way it is because of the
scheme of words
when you meet a man
you meet a scheme of words
patterns of concept
so if the scheme of words were changed
then man and planet earth would be
different
than what it is today
it is not that
the planet is wrong or man is wrong
it is just that
the scheme of words are not possible
to either man
or the planet

blessed be the dehydrated brain

is dreams sweeter than reality?
is reality less true than dreams since
dreams springs
from calls we thought in rebellion
wishful feeling
and spontaneity
reality boasts not of these without
hesitant thought
reality is sometimes nightmares more
than dreams
often in the deepest horror of a dream
one knows is a dream that one will awake
but of reality, one knows less and less as
time unfolds
as time erases days
one wishes to forget reality
hide ones head in the sand
stop one's ears from sound, stand up on
one's feet
and become strong then weak again
sink to the ground holding death's hand
oh comrade
if you are the father of great repose,
if you are all you seem and nothing more,
I'm glad that you are here
reality bruises me and beats, disowns me,
chokes my better self scared to dare
to breath
each breath may be its last
it has spent me in a life of this but

you'll adapt
oh friend, enfold everyone in your arms
lovingly,
tenderly you wrap each mind with night
shadows
you know man is better than the other
you'll give yourself completely to all
and your creed is integration and equality
in the dust
you are simplicity not confusion and
complexity of madness and despair
you're only one thing only not potential of
what you are,
death and finality is your aim
you do not pretend to be beautiful
silence is your speech
you're greater than the presence of
this world
mankind rushes to meet you
you're a master not slave
you're a marksman sure of yourself
who among them will refuse to bow
before your throne
sooner or later reluctant of the glare
you're the arch enemy of life
it can not see you
it knows not what you are, nor how to
conquer you
frightened, bewildered he lashes at the
empty air

but you see him you know him and mark
him from birth
sometime you claim him at birth
reality—
what say you
puny lad
what cause have you for being
you seek and search and search to find
that all you are
is overshadowed by
shadows by night

uncompromising annihilations
death is greater than life
blessed be the name of death
for in its hands
is perfect equality
for every man
damn these skins and creeds and stupid
beliefs that separated the millions of
tribes of men

blessed be the bones that lie
bleached in the sand,
the skeleton that hangs
dancing in the wind
blessed be the dehydrated brain
that can no longer persecute
and think evil thoughts
or perpetrate or perpetuate
evil deeds

blessed be these
for in the lack of life
or where there's not life
there's no pain and misery

there's no knowledge of death
or frustration or hate
or any of the stupid things
that clutter life so thoroughly
that it's not seen as a living force

only a figment of the mind
only a wish that should never
have taken thought
in the wistful mind of man

blessed be nothing in a vacuum
and things that should never have known
reality

yes, in the night I sit
in the lateness of the hour
I browse and write my thoughts

look forward into the night
upon its faint shadows
from another kind of world

illusions real or asleep

if there is today, or if there is the once
upon a time, what difference there
as now is patterned upon the unmoving
then
if the past then is not of natural is-ness,
not that I'd want to be
whatever is I am, what I am is
if I can change myself in life, then
monotony I do abdicate that monotony
give way to cascading variety
what is the meaning of this earth
kingdom, this kingdom of differential
heaven
what difference nothing
what difference everything
beware of this seeming light
beware of this seeming death
they unite in a cross, the world is not real
life only seems to be, death only seems
to be
the question is life death
but they are made to be disguised
synonyms
they are not of the natural equation
the equation is infinity
the Equation is the alternative reality
the equation is the duality of the duel
universe
what new thing teases my mind
what other things die in despair

am I really me or are you your self
do you have my place and I have yours,
what difference this
are we designs in a pattern or just a
pattern of something to come
are we truly real or illusions as life itself
or illusions as death itself or illusions real
but asleep of with deceptions in life
what are these things that puzzle me
I seek to shun them
they burn me
they torment me
they send me sailing
though the sky

what are these things?
are they more than I
or are we one
all of us one
you and I
one
the thoughts I have spoken
one
inseparably so
eternally so
is that the way things are
is that the truth for it
or is there something more
something more even
than eternity

something more
than the circle of everything
something more than anything
you ever dared to believe
to be true
let me remind those
who love the thing
and to all men who
in some future day
may wish to create another thing
in its stead
my soul shall tell the story
my soul shall sing its song
my soul is a living thing
for eyes to see
ears to hear
lips to speak
enforced from today
I dub its sword
invincible

the truth about planet earth

truth is bad
a truth is good
it depends upon where and why and how
and who you are
the truth about planet earth
is bad
the word truth must be considered
catholic
and the precepts of that which is called
truth must be equationized and balanced
and understood
or else
it must be a banner
and another truth placed in its place
this is the idea of the greater age of
outer worlds of otherness
this is the word from the cosmic cosmo
tomorrow

fast fading echoes

they taught me to share all I had
with them
I did
and got nothing in return
one day I found that because I did,
I died
then another tomorrow they never told
me of
came with the abruptness of a fiery gun
and spoke of cosmic equations
the equations of sight similarity
the equations of sound similarity
a secret code of eternal elasticity
clear only to those meant to live beyond
the law of earth
who must choose to understand the
meaning of the
death insurance
of cosmic surety
and use it as a shield against the
pretenders
of the fast-fading
echoes
of the damned
yesterdays

the secret code of eternal elasticity
clear only to those meant to live

beyond the law of earth
who must choose to understand
the meaning of the
death insurance
of cosmic surety
and use it as a shield against
the pretenders
of the fast-fading
echoes
of the damned
yesterdays
who must choose to understand
the meaning of the
death insurance
the death insurance
the death insurance of cosmic surety
and use it as a shield against the
pretenders
of the fast-fading
echoes
of the damned yesterdays

other planes of life

they cannot seem to accept me
because I'm not supposed to be real
they think they're the only real
they think that their way of life is the only
life
thus, instead of a friendly handshake or
mutual recognition
they pass me by
not caring to understand that I really am I
and that I'm truly being
and cosmically alive
if they would rise above their wisdom
they could see me as I am
and they would understand
that there are other planes of life
greater than the plane they know
all around them are other ways to greater
wisdom
but with eyes shut and ears closed
they listen to their inner voices within
the recorded voice of their abolished god
of the past

not a myth

whose reality are you
if you are not a myth
whose reality are you

if you are not a reality
whose myth are you

if you are not a reality
whose myth are you

if you are not a myth
whose reality are you

if you are not a myth
whose reality are you

like a universe

perfect?
if they only knew
what great jokes God has played on
humanity
yes, he's placed me in the midst of them
for vague purpose of vague and
yet so great that I don't know where
it is myself
I don't know where this purpose lies
hidden
what is there?
a soft fire that is burning within me
to let me know
yes, it's there
and my mind searches for it
and my heart searches for it
And I look and I think,
yes, here it is
then it's gone
it's like a mist
then it's like a sunset
it's like a sunrise
it's like a universe
it lies there
and yet I walk among people all long
not knowing
and the people not knowing
and then I think
I say,
what a great joke I am

and then, strangely enough
I look at people sometimes and I hate
them
I look at them and I hate them
I don't wish to destroy them
I don't want to harm them
But I hate them
Because I know that I'm a part of them
that I am here for them
that I belong to them
and that's why I hate them
because you see, if I didn't belong to them
if I wasn't placed here for them
I would be a free spirit
But I can't be free as long as I haven't
served my purpose
I can't be free as long as I give to people
what I have to give to them
yes, I'm more free than most men
I'm more free than most spirits
but yet I am chained
you see, it's a great joke on me, too
then again, I look at people, and I
love them
I love them so very much until I turn
my head in shame
I want to touch them with my fingertips
and erase the frown from their face
I want to touch them with my mind and
erase every care and every sorrow away

I want to touch them with my mind and
open their mind's eye and let them see
the things that I know and feel
I want to do that because I love them
then I look at them, then I hate them
again
I hate them because I love them so much
and I don't know
I don't know where hate begins and love
ends
I don't know how love ends and hate
begins
I don't know any of those things
all I know is
I'm a great joke
I'm the biggest joke that's ever been
played upon the world
and people think
they think that God has no ailment
but I know because I'm a living joke
I'm one that will cause people to scratch
their heads in wonderment
In search of their hollow hearts
and look in their souls and wonder,
Where did he come from? What is he?
Who made him?
You see, I'm such a great joke
until I tickle myself

I'm not to blame

I'm not to blame
and if I am
then I am to blame
then what— will that change things?
will that change the course of
the world?
their pardons and pains
I am not to blame
but if I am
I acknowledge it
and all I say is
it is lamentable
to bear blame and not share it
to feel blame
and no one could not avoid
the thing that lead to it
birds without wings
birds without wings
are they unaware there are no wings
where wings should be?
birds without wings
poised in tense takeoff
sailing
sailing unless they drop to earth
are they hurt?
bruised?
bewildered?
angry?
they rush to the takeoff place again
poised, tense, ready
go

strange aliens casting shadows

I was trying to find myself
find the idea from which I sprang
find thee, the forest where it lives
find the trees which I am alike
there are no roots for trees on city
pavements in ugly cities and blasé minds
let me find trees like myself
the same height as I
same kind as I that I might raise my limbs
in measures to the sky the same as they
trees of kindred spirit, trees attuned to
me whose leaves rustles with music
to the soft accompaniment of the wind
trees who do not drop me anywhere
hiding the sunlight from my face
trees to whom I am not a giant
unalike strange aliens casting
shadows in their way
trees that are not scrawny malcontent
inclined to otherness
trees that are themselves as I am myself
trees that I can call my living friends

tomorrow's realm

in some far-off place
many light years in space
I wait for you
where human feet have never trod
where human eyes have never seen
I'll build a world of abstract dreams
and wait for you
in tomorrow's realm
we'll take the helm
of a new ship
like the lash of a whip
we'll start on the way
and safely journey
to a new shore

pure music is your nemesis

that's what the music says
that is how I say:
the music

the music is a journey
the journey is endless
it is sound
endless-ness
communication language point
endless sound is a universal language
because that is what the music is
equations bridge across a
bridgeless
bottomless
world of sound
that is what the music is

a universal language
the bridge communication of sound
there is no other way to speak to
everyone in language
each of us can feel and understand
except for the music
there is no other way to speak to everyone
in language
each can understand
and feel
except
through
the music

how can you speak to other worlds
except through the music
the music lets them know where you are
and what you are
the music lets them know where you're at
and what you are
if you are pure
the music's pure
the music is your testing ground
it is your choice
that tells the tale
when all else fails
pure music is what you must face
if you limit
if you reject
if you do not consider
if you are selfish
earthly-bound
pure music is your nemesis
pure music is what you must face
if you limit
if you reject
if you do not consider
if you are selfish
earthly-bound
pure music is your nemesis
you cannot pretend
you will accept or you will reject
there is no middle ground
the mirror of pure music is a negative

field
that photographs the image mind
impression of soul and psychic self
in the potential immediate altered
destiny
the music
is the image
is the sound image
the living image of sound
image sound of the cosmo-world of
pushed journeys
the waves of sound are like waves of
water in the ocean
there is a tide in time of sound
this is the music
it is like a journey which is endless
unscheduled directions are suddenly
necessary
mind bent to synchronize the code of
momentum
dimensional to environmental light or
darkness equation
of balanced image or improvisational
alter-counterpoint
blueprint sound
the music is not only just music
it touches and projects other dimensions
time zone eternities
and cosmo infinities
spiraled parallels
the parallels are fields

fields of parables which are instruments
for the instruments are not only just
instruments
the people are the instruments
that's how the music goes
that is what the music is
that is the mirror on the wall
above the handwriting there
it is invisible to all
it is a mirror which you must hear
vibrations
rhythm
harmonic sound
is hidden in each melody
it is never what it seems to be
you can only hear what the mirror sees
no more, nor less is ever allowed
the sound mirror is what you see of
you
that sounds
if you are not sound
then you're not pure
pure is real sincerity
and pure knows pure is sound
and true
it's all what the music says of you
it's not what the music you say it is
it's all what the music says of you
the music is the living mirror of the
universe

the end

and so the world
comes to its end

but what is the end?

the end is
what they desire

every desire
is an end

and every end
is a desire

then
the end of the world
is a desire of the world

what type of end do you desire?

In November of 2010, Norton Records released three collections of unheard Sun Ra poetry entitled *Strange Worlds In My Mind*, *The Sub-Dwellers* and *The Outer Darkness*, which I had culled from the Archive. The discovery of these recordings was a sheer joy to me. Here were first take renditions - never before heard - which provided an inlet into the clairvoyant mind of Sun Ra through his recorded poems. This book includes selected recorded poetry from the Norton collections, plus transcriptions of several additional poems from 1957 to 1982, all with a decidedly otherworldly, extraterrestrial, intergalactic, hypernatural bent.

—Michael D. Anderson,
Executive Director of the
Sun Ra Music Archive

KICKS BOOKS PRESENTS...

Kicks Magazine Rock & Roll Photo Album #1
The Great Lost Photographs of Eddie Rocco

Fabulous collection of previously unpublished photographs by Charlton Publications photographer Eddie Rocco! Sepia-toned trade paperback includes photo tribute to Kicks icon Esquerita plus other favorites including Redd Foxx, Ruth Brown, the Treniers, Jackie Wilson, Johnny Otis, the Beach Boys, Jan & Dean, the Byrds and more!

KICKS PUBLISHING CO.

PO Box 646 Cooper Station, NY NY 10276

Gentlemen, I enclose ❑ check or ❑ money order, payment in full for books ordered. I understand that I may be so satisfied, I will need to come back and order more copies. All orders shipped media mail in USA. Foreign orders and others desiring payment via Paypal or credit card, kindly shop online at www.nortonrecords.com.

❑ Rocco book $10 postpaid in USA

Name ______________________________

Address ______________________________

City ______________ Zip __________ State ______

OTHER KICKS BOOKS
YOU WILL ENJOY

KB1 *Sweets and Other Stories* by Andre Williams
KB2 *This Planet is Doomed* by Sun Ra
KB3 *Save The Last Dance For Satan* by Nick Tosches
KB4 *Pulling A Train* by Harlan Ellison
KB5 *Tall Cool One* by Kim Fowley

WILLIAMS · SUN RA · TOSCHES · ELLISON · FOWLEY

KICKS BOOKS

PO BOX 646 COOPER STATION,
NEW YORK NY 10276
www.kicksbooks.com